Love,
Dina Heedeena
s

I Hope

by
Dina Nasr-Heerema

Illustrations by Claude Martinot

I Hope
Copyright 2014 © by Dina-Nasr-Heerema

ISBN 978-0-692-23844-8

Illustrations by Claude Martinot
Cover and text design by
Elizabeth Sheehan Graphic Design

First edition July 2014

To My Precious Jewel,
I loved you from the very start
You stole my breath
and embraced my heart.
Our life together has just begun
And forever you will be my sunshine!

I love you ya hayeteh!
Love, Mommy

One look from you and
I knew...my life had changed,
my wish had come true.

I watch you grow,
I watch you wonder and
hope you never fail to keep
your thunder.

I hope you love each and every day and you never lose your sense of play.

I hope that everything
you see makes you question why
and how it came to be.

I hope that you will always keep
that burning flame that shines
from way down deep.

I hope when hard times come your way, you stand strong....

and believe in the start of a new day.

I hope that you will strive to be
the best person for the world to see.

I hope all your dreams
come true, just like mine did
when I had you.

The day will come when
I'll say goodbye but don't cry...

my sweet sunshine...

Take these hopes I have for you
and pass them along to your
little one...pink or blue!

Dina Nasr-Heerema; author of "A Twist of Fate", was inspired by her daughter Jewel's sense of wonder and amazement, to write this rhyming book of hopes that a mother has for her child.

Dina teaches elementary school and is inspired by children every day. She lives in New Jersey with her husband Rich and their precious daughter Jewel.

CPSIA information can be obtained
at www.ICGtesting.com
Printed in the USA
BVXC01n1824240814
363835BV00001B/1